AF228154

WEAPONS OF WORLD WAR II

BY EMMA KAISER

CONTENT CONSULTANT
Brian K. Feltman, PhD
Professor of History
Georgia Southern University

Cover image: The M4 Sherman tank was an important weapon used by Allied forces during World War II.

Core Library

An Imprint of Abdo Publishing
abdobooks.com

abdobooks.com

Published by Abdo Publishing, a division of ABDO, PO Box 398166, Minneapolis, Minnesota 55439. Copyright © 2025 by Abdo Consulting Group, Inc. International copyrights reserved in all countries. No part of this book may be reproduced in any form without written permission from the publisher. Core Library™ is a trademark and logo of Abdo Publishing.

Printed in the United States of America, North Mankato, Minnesota.
052024
092024

Cover Photo: Camerique/Archive Photos/Getty Images
Interior Photos: Archive Photos/Getty Images, 4–5; AFP/Getty Images, 6, 12; Bettmann/Getty Images, 8, 32–33, 43; Lt. J. A. Hampton/Imperial War Museums/Getty Images, 11; GL Archive/Alamy, 14–15; Sgt. Joanna Bradshaw/Ohio National Guard/DVIDS, 16; Gunnery Sgt. Rome Lazarus/US Marine Corps/DVIDS, 19; Daily Herald Archive/National Science & Media Museum/SSPL/Getty Images, 22–23, 45; Sovfoto/Universal Images Group/Getty Images, 25; Universal History Archive/Universal Images Group/Getty Images, 27 (top); Niday Picture Library/Alamy, 27 (middle); The Keasbury-Gordon Photograph Archive/KGPA Ltd/Alamy, 27 (bottom); Kevin Sawford/imageBROKER.com GmbH & Co. KG/Alamy, 29; Corbis Historical/Getty Images, 30, 39 (bottom); Manchester Daily Express/SSPL/Getty Images, 34; MPI/Archive Photos/Getty Images, 39 (top)

Editor: Marley Richmond
Series Designer: Ryan Gale

Library of Congress Control Number: 2023949172

Publisher's Cataloging-in-Publication Data

Names: Kaiser, Emma, author.
Title: Weapons of world war II / by Emma Kaiser
Description: Minneapolis, Minnesota: Abdo Publishing, 2025 | Series: World war II | Includes online resources and index.
Identifiers: ISBN 9781098293673 (lib. bdg.) | ISBN 9798384912941 (ebook)
Subjects: LCSH: World War, 1939-1945--Juvenile literature. | Military supplies--Juvenile literature. | Military weapons--Juvenile literature. | Equipment and supplies--Juvenile literature. | Arms transfers--Juvenile literature. | Weapons industry--Juvenile literature. | Politics and government--Juvenile literature.
Classification: DDC 940.53--dc23

CONTENTS

WEAPONS OF WAR

The attack began at about midnight on June 6, 1944. Thousands of US and British troops were preparing to parachute into the northern region of France. More than 1,200 planes, including Douglas C-47s, were filled with soldiers waiting for the signal to jump. Some soldiers were throwing up because they were so scared. When a green light flashed, the soldiers leaped into the night with a *whoosh*.

As the troops' parachutes opened, some were jerked so hard that their helmets or packs

Troops prepared to parachute into France on June 6, 1944. Some soldiers darkened their faces to blend into their surroundings.

were torn off. The sky filled with the crackle of gunfire. German troops below were using machine guns to fire at the soldiers and planes. Bullets tore through the soldiers' parachutes. Fighter planes dropped bombs, which started fires on the ground below. The air was thick with the smell of gunpowder and smoke. The night was lit up like a fireworks display.

Not all the men survived the jump. Those who did landed in Normandy, France. The soldiers landed in fields and in pastures. Some were unlucky enough to land in trees or in water. Many had to use knives to cut themselves out of their harnesses. Some suffered injuries from hard landings. But these men had a job to do. They had to attack their opponents so that troops soon landing on the beaches of Normandy stood a better chance of success.

D-DAY

World War II (1939–1945) had been raging in Europe since September 1, 1939. On one side of the war were the Axis powers, including Germany, Italy, and Japan. They fought the Allied powers, including the United States, the United Kingdom, and the Soviet Union. During the war, Germany had been expanding its territory across Europe. Adolf Hitler and the Nazi Party led Germany as it occupied other countries, including France. The Allied forces had arrived in Normandy to liberate France. Allied leaders hoped that this battle would be the first step toward stopping German expansion and freeing countries under Germany's control. The invasion of Normandy was officially called Operation Overlord. It is also known as D-Day.

Higgins boats brought soldiers from larger ships to the beaches of Normandy. These boats could also transport vehicles such as tanks.

As the Allied troops were parachuting into France, nearly 7,000 ships were making their way to five different beaches on the Normandy coast. These included naval combat ships, battleships, supply ships, and ships carrying soldiers to shore. Allied soldiers arrived on the beaches in ships called Higgins boats. These boats were plated in armor and had ramps for easier exit. Approximately 30 men could fit in a Higgins boat, and soldiers crouched down and kept their heads low to avoid gunfire. The air was full of planes whirring overhead. Germans fired powerful MG42 machine guns from cliffs overlooking the beaches. Allied battleships fired back from the water.

Approximately 6.5 million mines had been placed in the water and on the beaches by German defenses. These mines exploded when hit or stepped on.

The beaches were full of chaos and wounded men. The only way to stay alive was to keep moving.

A TURNING POINT IN THE WAR

D-Day was an important turning point in World War II. It was the largest amphibious invasion in recorded history. More than 150,000 Allied soldiers were part of the invasion. D-Day led to the Allied forces pushing the Germans out of France and other occupied nations. The Allies would eventually

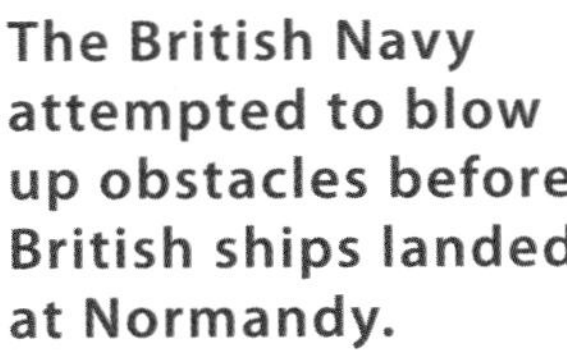

secure Germany's surrender. Some historians refer to D-Day as the beginning of the end of the war.

The Battle of Normandy officially ended when the Allied forces reached Paris and liberated France at the end of August 1944. More than 100,000 troops were killed over the course of the battle. Thousands of French civilians were also killed in bombings.

World War II led to advancements and inventions in weapons and warfare. Many types of weapons, such as those used on D-Day, were needed to fight battles on land, at sea, and in the air. The kinds of weapons each military used often meant the difference between

Allied forces drove an M4 Sherman tank through Paris to celebrate the city's liberation.

victory and defeat. Weapons could also mean the difference between life and death. From tanks and fighter planes to guns and bombs, many weapons from World War II changed the way wars were fought in the future.

STRAIGHT TO THE
SOURCE

DeWitt Lowrey was part of the US 101st Airborne Division. He parachuted into Normandy. He said:

> *I didn't hit the ground. I hit a tree and hung there. It was a big old tree . . . and I could see two machine guns in each corner of a field shooting at me. Those bullets just whizzed past me through those leaves and branches. It sounded like they were firing at a barn. . . . My buddies took care of the machine guns. . . . I cut my ammo off my leg and let it drop, let my machine gun drop, then got myself out of the harness, and that's the way I came down.*

> Source: Kevin M. Hymel. "The WW2 Paratrooper: First-Hand Accounts of the D-Day Invasion." *Warfare History Network*, n.d., warfarehistorynetwork.com. Accessed 12 Sept. 2023.

CONSIDER YOUR AUDIENCE

Adapt this passage for a different audience, such as your principal or friends. Write a short story conveying this same information for the new audience. How does your passage differ from the original text and why?

FIREARMS

Firearms were the primary weapons of infantry soldiers. Firearms are weapons that shoot bullets at powerful speeds. Most firearms are made to be carried by a single person. Infantry soldiers marched and fought on foot. Without a vehicle, they needed to carry their own weapons. There were many kinds of firearms a soldier might use. Each weapon had a different role in battle.

RIFLES

A rifle is a firearm that is fired from the shoulder. Its long barrel has grooves called rifling inside to help the gun shoot straight

US Marines used the Thompson submachine gun during the Battle of Okinawa.

M1 Garand rifles have been replaced in battle. But these weapons are still used in ceremonies.

and accurately. Rifles can hit targets that are far away, so soldiers use them at long range in combat.

The M1 Garand rifle was one of the most well-recognized weapons used during World War II. It was the standard rifle used by the US Army and the first standard-issue semiautomatic military rifle. When a semiautomatic gun is fired, the next bullet is automatically loaded in the weapon. Before these firearms, soldiers had to load each bullet into their guns by hand, reloading after each shot. Semiautomatic weapons allowed soldiers to fire more rounds more quickly.

Another significant rifle was the German Sturmgewehr 44. Its name means "storm rifle" in German. This firearm became the world's first assault rifle. That means it could switch between semiautomatic and fully automatic fire. When the gun was semiautomatic, it would fire one bullet each

time the trigger was pulled. In automatic mode, it fired
bullets continuously when the trigger was held down.

HANDGUNS

Unlike rifles, handguns can be held and fired with
one hand. They aren't as powerful as rifles, but they
are easier to conceal. They are also easier to shoot at
closer range.

The Germans used the Luger pistol. The Colt 1911
handgun was the standard US service pistol during
World War II. It was designed for accuracy and ease
of use. The Soviet Union created its own semiautomatic
pistol called the Tokarev TT-33.

MACHINE GUNS

A machine gun is an automatic weapon that can fire
many rounds of ammunition very quickly. It will continue
to fire as long as the trigger is held down and the gun
has ammunition. This makes machine guns very deadly
weapons. During World War II, many machine guns

Some militaries still use the MG42 machine gun.

were placed on stands and required multiple soldiers to operate them.

The MG42 was a famous machine gun used by the Germans. It was cheap and easy to build but also reliable. It could fire 1,200 rounds per minute, which was far more than the Allied forces' guns could shoot.

Submachine guns were also popular weapons during World War II. Submachine guns are often smaller and slightly less powerful than machine guns. But they are easier for individual soldiers to operate. The United States and many of the other Allied forces used the Thompson submachine gun. It was also known as the Tommy gun. The British used the Sten submachine gun. It had a simple design and was easy to produce. More than 4 million were made during the 1940s.

FLAMETHROWERS

A flamethrower is a weapon that shoots out flaming oil or gasoline. These weapons could be carried by soldiers or installed in tanks. The most powerful flamethrowers could reach about 300 feet (90 m). British and US flamethrowers, such as the M1 flamethrower, used napalm as fuel. This is a type of thickened gasoline. Napalm shot farther and burned hotter than regular gas. It also stuck to everything it touched and continued to burn.

ANTITANK WEAPONS

Tanks became more powerful during World War II, so armies had to come up with new weapons to fight them. These were known as antitank weapons. The US military developed the M1 rocket launcher. This weapon was also called the bazooka.

The bazooka was a long metal tube that could fire a 3.5-pound (1.6-kg) rocket. Bazookas were used on D-Day and helped fight the Germans in France. The British developed the Projector, Infantry, Anti-Tank (PIAT) gun. It was more powerful than the bazooka, but it was heavier and more difficult to fire.

The Germans' antitank weapon was called the Panzerschreck, which means "tank terror." The Panzerschreck was more powerful than the bazooka. But troops had to be close to their target. The weapon's range was only about 500 feet (150 m).

EXPLORE ONLINE

Chapter Two talks about firearms used by the Allied and Axis forces. The machine gun was one type of firearm that was important in the war. The article at the website below goes into more depth on machine guns. Does the article answer any of the questions you had about this kind of weapon?

MACHINE GUN

abdocorelibrary.com/weapons-world-war-ii

VEHICLES

Military vehicles are machines capable of transporting soldiers and supplies. But they can also be used as weapons. Military vehicles are used in battles on land, at sea, and in the sky. They include machines such as tanks and aircraft. Often they are designed with armor to keep the vehicles and soldiers safe. They are also armed with weapons to attack opponents.

TANKS

Tanks were used by many countries during World War II and had a huge impact in battle. Tanks are large, heavily armored land vehicles.

The British Supermarine Spitfire was an important plane during World War II. The aircraft had eight machine guns.

They move on looped chains called tracks, which allow them to travel over rough terrain. They can easily drive over bumpy ground and cross holes and trenches. Tanks are also armed with powerful guns and explosives.

The German Tiger tanks were some of the most powerful tanks produced during the war. They were fitted with artillery guns that could penetrate other tanks' armor from up to 3,280 feet (1,000 m) away. Tiger tanks were massive and weighed up to 70 tons (64 metric tons). They had very thick armor that kept soldiers safe inside. Following the invasion of Normandy, German tanks helped stop an Allied plan called Operation Goodwood. This mission would have allowed Allied troops to continue past the beaches where they landed. German tanks destroyed hundreds of the Allies' tanks and temporarily prevented them from moving forward into France.

The Allies also had powerful tanks of their own. The M4 Sherman Firefly tank was used mainly by the British and Canadian armies. It was fast firing and one of the

Soviet T-34 tanks drove through Berlin, Germany, as World War II in Europe came to an end.

few tanks powerful enough to penetrate the Tiger tank's armor during the Battle of Normandy. The Russian T-34 tank also played a big role in the Soviet Union's battles against Germany. The T-34 was versatile and well armed. It was also produced in large numbers. This gave the Soviet Union an advantage over Germany.

SHIPS

World War II battles were not limited to land. They were fought in the Atlantic and Pacific Oceans as well. Battleships were large, heavy ships covered in armor. They had powerful guns that could hit targets that

DUKW VEHICLES

DUKW vehicles, also called ducks, were 2.5-ton (2.3-metric ton) six-wheeled trucks. They were amphibious. This meant they could be used in the water and on land. They were shaped like boats and could reach speeds of approximately 5.5 miles per hour (8.9 km/h) at sea. On land, their top speed was 50 miles per hour (80 km/h). DUKW vehicles were often used to carry troops, weapons, supplies, and ammunition. They played a role in the Allied forces' success during the invasion of Normandy.

were miles away. The *Yamato* was a famous Japanese battleship. At 65,000 tons (59,000 metric tons), it was much bigger than the US military's largest battleship. It also had the largest guns ever built for a warship.

Battles were also fought from beneath the surface of the water. The German U-boat was a kind of submarine. It could fire torpedoes from underwater that hit ships carrying supplies to Allied forces. U-boats were very successful in destroying enemy ships and traveling undetected. U-boats would often travel in groups and attack at night.

TYPES OF
SHIPS

Both the Allied and Axis forces used different types of ships. Battleships, aircraft carriers, and submarines were each important in battle. What types of missions would be best suited to each type of ship?

BATTLESHIPS

Example: *Yamato* (Japanese Imperial Navy)

Uses: Attacking enemies using powerful guns

AIRCRAFT CARRIERS

Example: USS *Enterprise* (US Navy)

Uses: Transporting aircraft and serving as a moveable landing strip

SUBMARINES

Example: U-boat (German Navy)

Uses: Stealth attacks from underwater

Another important type of ship during World War II was the aircraft carrier. Aircraft carriers are large ships that transport aircraft. Planes can then take off and land on these ships in the middle of the ocean. The USS *Enterprise* was an important US aircraft carrier during World War II. It was used in many battles against the Empire of Japan in the Pacific.

PLANES

Planes also became crucial weapons used in World War II. The war led to many

The German
Messerschmitt
Bf 109 was armed
with two machine
guns and a cannon.

developments in aircraft and aviation. Planes became much faster and more powerful.

Fighter planes were used for combat in the air. They were fast and easy to maneuver. One of the deadliest planes of World War II was the German Messerschmitt Bf 109. It was fitted with machine guns, rockets, and bombs. It could reach speeds of about 400 miles per hour (640 km/h). A German pilot named Erich Hartmann was known for his deadly skill in the air. He shot down 352 enemies while flying the Bf 109.

One of the only planes that could challenge the German Bf 109 was the British Supermarine Spitfire.

Enola Gay was the name of the plane that US forces used to drop the first atomic bomb on Hiroshima, Japan.

It had a sleek design that made it especially fast in the air. It was known for being able to take damage and continue to fly. It also had eight machine guns that made it deadly for land targets and other planes.

In the Pacific, the skies were ruled by Japan's Mitsubishi A6M Zero. This fighter plane was lightweight, fast, and highly maneuverable. It led many air strikes during attacks on China. It was also used in the bombing of the US naval base at Pearl Harbor on

December 7, 1941. The base was in Hawaii. The United States joined World War II after this bombing.

Many planes made a difference during the war, but one plane may have had the biggest effect. That was the US military's Boeing B-29 Superfortress. It was a bomber, which was a type of airplane used to transport and drop explosives. The B-29 was one of the biggest bombers of the time. It could carry bombs over long distances. Two B-29 planes dropped the atomic bombs on Japan that ended the war.

FURTHER EVIDENCE

Chapter Three covers types of tanks used during World War II. What was one of the main points of this section? What evidence is included to support this point? Read the article at the website below. Does the information on the website support the main point of the chapter? Does it present new evidence?

TANKS REIGNED SUPREME ON WORLD WAR II BATTLEFIELDS

abdocorelibrary.com/weapons-world-war-ii

BOMBS AND EXPLOSIVES

Bombing was a major military strategy of World War II. Bomb raids involved air forces dropping large explosives on enemy territory. Bombs were used to weaken the enemies' forces. Common bomb targets included factories, railroads, and military bases. But many cities and civilian populations were also targets of bombings.

BOMB ATTACKS

Allied forces began an air raid on Hamburg, Germany, on July 24, 1943. Great Britain's

Allied forces destroyed much of Dresden, Germany, during an air raid in February 1945. The attack killed an estimated 35,000 people.

The Royal Air Force Lancaster bomber plane could carry up to 14,000 pounds (6,350 kg) of bombs.

Royal Air Force dropped more than 350,000 incendiary bombs on the first day alone. Incendiary bombs are made to catch on fire. Many used napalm. They caused the city to burn. Soon US forces joined the bombing.

Their planes also dropped incendiary bombs on military targets in Hamburg.

One important type of British armor-piercing bomb was called the Grand Slam. Grand Slam bombs each weighed 22,000 pounds (10,000 kg). They were designed to penetrate hard materials such as concrete. A Grand Slam bomb was used on a railroad bridge in Bielefeld, Germany. The explosive created a massive crater and left the route unusable by German forces.

One of the German explosives was the V-1 flying bomb. The V-1 had a range of 150 miles (241 km), and it could steer itself to a target. German forces fired these bombs from France into London, England. The V-1 paved the way for more advanced missiles used in later wars.

Japan used several kinds of bombs against the US naval base at Pearl Harbor. It dropped many Type 91 torpedoes into the water from aircraft. These torpedoes penetrated ships and exploded underwater. Most US ships that were sunk during the attack were destroyed by torpedoes. Japanese forces also used a Type 98 land bomb. This was a more general-purpose bomb that was used to destroy aircraft on land.

THE ATOMIC BOMB

During World War II, the United States created a type of bomb that had never been used before. It was called the atomic bomb. Atomic bombs are a type of nuclear weapon. Their power comes from fission. Fission is the process of splitting an atom, which releases an enormous amount of energy. Atomic bombs use the fission of uranium or plutonium to create explosions. J. Robert Oppenheimer was a scientist who led the US project to develop the first atomic bomb, codenamed the Manhattan Project.

The US military was the first to use atomic bombs in warfare. US president Harry S. Truman believed that using atomic bombs would end the war quickly. But it was not a decision he made lightly. Truman knew

CREATING THE BOMB

J. Robert Oppenheimer was proud of his achievement in building the atomic bomb. He was glad the United States developed the weapon before the Germans did. He felt he had a duty to his country, but he also struggled with guilt. After the United States dropped atomic bombs on Japan, Oppenheimer told US president Harry S. Truman, "I have blood on my hands." Oppenheimer worried about the possibility of a future nuclear war. He worried that more lives would be lost and worked to prevent the development of more powerful nuclear weapons. However, Oppenheimer never apologized for his role in creating the atomic bombs dropped on Japan.

the bombs would kill thousands of people, including civilians. Truman considered other options, such as invading Japan. But an invasion would kill millions of people. He ultimately decided that using atomic bombs was the best option.

The US Army Air Forces dropped an atomic bomb called Little Boy on Hiroshima, Japan, on August 6, 1945. The explosion immediately devastated 4.4 square miles (11 sq km) of the city. More than 80,000 people were killed instantly. About 63 percent of the city's structures were destroyed.

The United States dropped a second atomic bomb, called Fat Man, three days later on August 9. This bomb was dropped on the Japanese city of Nagasaki. Another 40,000 people were instantly killed in this explosion. The force of the bomb was equal to 21,000 tons (19,000 metric tons) of TNT.

Atomic bombs release radiation after the initial explosion. This is a harmful type of energy that can cause long-term health problems for people who survive

THE TWO ATOMIC
BOMBS

Little Boy and Fat Man were different kinds of atomic bombs. Little Boy needed much more fuel than Fat Man, and it was still not as powerful. But they both produced much larger explosions than if they were fueled by TNT, which is a common explosive. Think about the destruction caused by each of the bombs. Does this comparison help you understand how they impacted the cities that they hit?

LITTLE BOY

Fuel type: Uranium
Amount of fuel: 140 pounds (63.5 kg)
Force of explosion: Equal to 15,000 tons (13,610 metric tons) of TNT

FAT MAN

Fuel type: Plutonium
Amount of fuel: 13.6 pounds (6 kg)
Force of explosion: Equal to 21,000 tons (19,000 metric tons) of TNT

the bombing. By the end of 1945, the impact and aftermath of the two atomic bombs would result in the deaths of more than 210,000 people.

After the United States dropped both atomic bombs, Japan began negotiating for surrender. Germany and Italy had already surrendered. World War II officially ended on September 2, 1945.

The advancements in weapons made during the war changed the world forever. The improvement of semiautomatic and automatic firearms changed how guns were made. Aircraft became more powerful and used better technology. The atomic bomb would change the way all countries approached future conflicts. Nuclear weapons became the most powerful weapon ever created or used. The United States began to make more of them, and many other countries raced to create their own. These weapons have a legacy that stretches far beyond World War II.

STRAIGHT TO THE
SOURCE

Emiko Okada survived the bombing of Hiroshima. She described her experience:

I was eight when the bomb dropped. My older sister was 12. She left early that morning to work on a [building] site and never came home. My parents searched for her for months and months. They never found her remains. . . .

I too was affected by the radiation and vomited profusely after the bomb attack. My hair fell out, my gums bled, and I was too ill to attend school. My grandmother lamented the suffering of her children and grandchildren and prayed. "How cruel, how so very cruel, if only it weren't for the [atomic bomb] . . ."

Source: Lily Rothman. "After the Bomb." *TIME*, n.d., time.com. Accessed 5 Sept. 2023.

WHAT'S THE BIG IDEA?

Take a close look at this passage. What is the author's main point? How was she affected by the atomic bomb? What is the author's perspective on using this type of weapon in war?

IMPORTANT DATES

September 1, 1939
World War II begins in Europe.

December 7, 1941
Japan bombs the US naval base at Pearl Harbor. The United States joins World War II shortly after.

July 24, 1943
Allied forces begin an air raid against Hamburg, Germany.

June 6, 1944
Allied forces invade Normandy during D-Day.

August 6, 1945
The US Army Air Forces drop the atomic bomb Little Boy on Hiroshima, Japan.

August 9, 1945
The US Army Air Forces drop the atomic bomb Fat Man on Nagasaki, Japan.

September 2, 1945

World War II ends with Japan's surrender.

STOP AND THINK

Tell the Tale

Chapter One of this book discusses a soldier's experience parachuting into France during the invasion of Normandy. Imagine you are also jumping out of a plane into battle. Write 200 words about what you encounter on your mission. What are the goals of your mission?

Surprise Me

Chapter Three discusses types of vehicles used in World War II. After reading this book, what two or three facts about war vehicles did you find most surprising? Write a few sentences about each fact. Why did you find each fact surprising?

Take a Stand

US leaders wanted to develop atomic weapons before other countries did. They believed dropping the atomic bomb would lead to the end of the war. Do you think it was right for the United States to create and use nuclear weapons? Do you think it should have acted differently? Why or why not?

Another View

This book talks about the use of bombs during World War II.
As you know, every source is different. Ask a librarian or
another adult to help you find another source about this
event. Write a short essay comparing and contrasting the
new source's point of view with that of this book's author.
What is the point of view of each author? How are they
similar and why? How are they different and why?

GLOSSARY

amphibious
related to both land and water

artillery
weapons used to fire missiles

atom
the smallest particles that make up matter

aviation
operating aircraft

catalyst
something that brings on an event or reaction

civilian
a person who is not in the military

fuse
a cord on a bomb that is lit to make the bomb explode

liberate
to free from enemy control

nuclear weapons
bombs powered by the energy released when an atom is split

remains
a dead body

torpedo
a weapon used against ships

versatile
has many uses

ONLINE RESOURCES

To learn more about the weapons of World War II, visit our free resource websites below.

Visit **abdocorelibrary.com** or scan this QR code for free Common Core resources for teachers and students, including vetted activities, multimedia, and booklinks, for deeper subject comprehension.

Visit **abdobooklinks.com** or scan this QR code for free additional online weblinks for further learning. These links are routinely monitored and updated to provide the most current information available.

LEARN MORE

Brallier, Jess M. *What Was the Bombing of Hiroshima?* Penguin Workshop, 2020.

Huddleston, Emma. *How the Bomb Changed Everything.* Abdo, 2022.

INDEX

About the Author

Emma Kaiser is a writer and educator based in western Minnesota. She has a master of fine arts in creative writing from the University of Minnesota, and her writing has been in a number of magazines and publications. She is the author of several other nonfiction books for students.